"It may not be 'always true that a good son // dies and a bad one punishes his father by living,' but what if that's how it feels, and you're that son? In the wrenchingly tender poems of *So Tall It Ends in Heaven*, Jayme Ringleb speaks from the living wound that thrives in the shadow of childhood abandonment; the poems trace the edges of that wound as Ringleb contemplates what it means to have equated a father with God, and to have defined oneself according to the wishes of another: 'But I thought want was / wooden, simple: whatever He wanted, that's what I was.' As they take us through the harrowing 'garden / of swaying fathers,' Ringleb's poems at once confront and enact how the hurt that haunts us has everything to do with how we grow up to love, if we can at all, someone else: brokenly, tentatively, and as if our lives depended on it—as I believe they do. These poems convince me of that. This is a hard-won, triumphant debut."

—CARL PHILLIPS, author of *Then the War*

"Countless very good first books of poetry enter the world each year, but only a fraction of a fraction are as mature, assured, or ambitiously realized as Jayme Ringleb's *So Tall It Ends in Heaven*. A peacock wails, the devil taps at the window, and young boys anoint each other in charcoal. Ringleb possesses that rarest triumvirate fluency of ear, heart, and mind that you find in the great poets of any era, any place—one poem here ends, 'We sleep / in a snarl, like lovers found in snow.' Another, 'It's almost a heaven, / neglecting you.' It's thrilling to discover a book you know you'll revisit for the rest of your life. These poems are better than good—they're undeniable."

—KAVEH AKBAR, author of *Pilgrim Bell*

"Jayme Ringleb is a master of the recursive, of writing that perfects the art of reach and return. These hushed and impeccable poems venture out, toward the figure of the father, toward the figure of the lover, toward the figure of the wayward man. And then they come back, bearing haunting revelations and a beauty that cuts deep. *So Tall It Ends in Heaven* is a tremendous book."

—NATALIE SHAPERO, author of *Popular Longing*

"In his brilliant poetry debut, *So Tall It Ends in Heaven*, Jayme Ringleb flawlessly renders both the macro and the micro wonders of the universe. He shows us the glory of galaxies seen through a Walmart telescope and the magic of fungus gnats appearing as if from thin air. Some poems in this collection read like parables, others, like prayers, and each one urges us to recognize the importance of mindful solitude and the healing that comes from letting go."

—PAIGE LEWIS, author of *Space Struck*

Published by Tin House, Portland, Oregon

Distributed by W. W. Norton & Company

Library of Congress Cataloging-in-Publication Data

Names: Ringleb, Jayme, 1985- author.
Title: So tall it ends in heaven / Jayme Ringleb.
Description: Portland, Oregon : Tin House, [2022]
Identifiers: LCCN 2022014527 | ISBN 9781953534408 (paperback) |
  ISBN 9781953534484 (ebook)
Subjects: LCGFT: Poetry.
Classification: LCC PS3618.I5399 S6 2022 | DDC 811/.6—dc23/eng/20220408
LC record available at https://lccn.loc.gov/2022014527

First US Edition 2022
Printed in the USA
Interior design by Jakob Vala

www.tinhouse.com

SO TALL IT ENDS IN HEAVEN

JAYME RINGLEB

TIN HOUSE / Portland, Oregon

CONTENTS

Maybe You Are a Certain Man

Maybe you want a good man
to keep   a man, it happens,
with a troublesome neighbor, a neighbor
with a dog. A good dog.

And the neighbor smokes too much,
one night falls asleep smoking,
and his mattress goes up.
Soon the room.

Still the dog won't leave.
It paces, bellyaching in the hall.
But your good man, no doubt, bounds in.
And you are there, frozen

out on the lawn without even
words to help. Maybe
he's got the dog slung
over his shoulders,

maybe he's kicking out walls,
he's finding a way back,
all ragged and covered in slag.
Maybe you want a good man,

but you will have to break him.
You will have to
make fire and, like a dog,
wake him in the night

only to reassure him you are there.
He must be certain
you are always there, with him,
in the burning house.

My Husband, Lost in the Wild

He said he buried
his right eye in South Georgia—

on a dare, he said,
when he was little, beneath

one green ash of two
that mark the end of a road

whose name he's
by now forgotten: *Lonesome*

something, maybe *Dog*
or *Cricket*. He said

he couldn't love me, not
really, not without

his old right eye,
and anyway, he'd left

his tongue as a tip
slid under a mug

at a small North Florida diner,
would collect it, too,

along the way, seeing
as he'd asked the server

to save it, and she had kindly
agreed. Three of his ribs

were further gone—one in Wisconsin,
where he'd planted it like a tree,

though he believed even then
nothing would bloom.

Another he pawned in Manitoba
for a silver bracelet,

which he wore only
when he was very sad,

and his last rib
he'd been keeping

in a safe deposit box
in a credit union

on the alien Oregon coast
where he'd visit sometimes,

stopping often at vantages
to take in expanses of pine

covered in moss
and something else, like brine;

and the pines were tall,
tall and uncommunicating,

as if they had been designed
only to listen. His ears

he'd left with me;
I told them

everything—words
I had invented for the texture

of new moons, city names
I had given to four slender

ant colonies that had since
emerged on the lawn.

I told the ears *Come back to me*,
but they were unable to

relay these types of things,
and anyway there was nothing

else to do. I took all
my tiniest veins

and pitched them
as a woven tightrope

out the kitchen window
and hooked, with

a makeshift grapple, the cheek
of the visible moon, which

carried me away, and I was sorry
to have wounded it like that,

and I was sorry to be carried
by what I had wounded.

I Was, of Course

God once made me a raft of cedars,

                               rowed with me one night

past the clean, barbed reef until His back, from an old outrage,

gave out.

               Beside the raft, plankton, dizzied in a snaggle

of moonlight, pinkened the sea, which otherwise seemed without

form. God grew

                  frightened and, as I retreated us to our

low island, said to me, *Stay quiet*

                         and *Be mine*. There, with

the simple trees, I was, of course,

                       always quiet, I was

already His. But God felt stranded, so He commanded

I make the raft into fire. He sat breaking cedar planks

in His hands

                while I built the fire tall, taller than a man.

When my God stepped into it, He paused, reconsidering

me, and then steadied Himself
                            as if boarding a small boat.

He told me, *You know I wanted you.* But I thought want was

wooden, simple:
                whatever He wanted, that's what I was.

Mutius in the Garden of Rejection

And with my sword I'll keep this door safe.

—Mutius, *Titus Andronicus*

There are five biblical gardens of significance, but more than twenty-
five gardens of significance in Rome

buried under other gardens of significance in Rome.

The biblical gardens of significance have not been buried, but God
has closed some of them.

There are no lyrebirds in Rome, but if there were, they would roost
mostly in the Vatican's English garden and mimic the Fountain
of the Eagle's fixed hiss.

Lyrebirds are doltish songsters who, closed in a fox's mouth, go limp
even before the scrap is done.

Here are the major facts: lyrebirds must roost in low branches, unable
as they are, like chickens, to fly for very long,

and Mutius is given twenty-five words before his father casually kills
him with a sword.

Meanwhile, the Cantonese slang *25 boy* means "traitor." A small
coincidence.

Another: in my country, 2.5 is the percent of killings that are filicides.

Three of Mutius's last twenty-five words—two of his last three—are the word *help*.

The five significant gardens of the Bible are the Garden of Rebellion, the Garden of Rejection, the Garden of Redemption, the Garden of Reception, and the Garden of Rejoicing. So many "Re-"s. As if the Bible keeps trying to get gardens right.

Twenty-five, in biblical terms, signifies grace multiplied by grace— "Grace upon grace"—which to some Christians means God calls back his children by killing 100 percent of them.

Beside the temple in the Villa Borghese gardens, I bend down to dig. The uncovered soil smells like burnt olives, and I wield a toy spade

with the other tourists, revealing a fake archeological site:

buried gardens of the real Lucius Licinius Lucullus, who has, we're told, been memorialized by a strain of Swiss chard—a mild and sweet strain, one that holds well after cutting.

In my edition of *Titus Andronicus*, the stage direction is "Stabbing MUTIUS," but my edition of *Titus Andronicus* does not specify the number of times Mutius is stabbed.

My father knows why five is the biblical number for grace, and he
    knows how to multiply grace by grace, but I do not.

I dig in the foreign garden, where I want a lyrebird to be,

and a fox—a fox who knows the lyrebird can fly, but not for long, and
    that it can live for twenty-five years, but rarely does.

Love Poem to the Son My Father Wished For

If I pause some nights when the sky seems
particularly simple, the air barely carrying
wafts of the neighbor's constant bonfires,
the stars rubbed clean of their dull texture, if I
pause to name the stars, as if by naming them
I could love them more, I feel closer to you—

even if it's too easy to love the stars, the way
telling me what you've done to roughen your hands
would be easy, or how you taught your daughters
to drag after you a workshop trolley
in the garage, naming all the pretty car parts—
caliper, strut dust sleeve, chassis. I don't know

what there is between a woman and a man,
but you know how to make the body submissive
and brave: when your father's God asks you
to heat something small and metal—a ball bearing, maybe
a fishhook or drywall nail—over a fire, to keep it in fire
until it glows, and then to swallow it, you do. I love

your mouth for this, its coarsenesses, scabbed
edges, numb scars—your father's God has demanded
so much of you. And now the burn-pitted tongue
tastes nothing, would taste nothing
even if the mouth bent down to kiss me, if only
to feel for a moment whether kisses could injure

better than gods. I have opened my mouth
to God, but only men enter. I imagine them
in their homes, milling, busying themselves
with cookware, working to assemble new,
oily-grated grills, or just standing in the drive,
as I imagine you do some nights, having

bedded a wife and left a robe she loves
folded over the wardrobe door, then slipping out,
finally, in our grandfather's mackinaw coat,
for a secret smoke, thinking sometimes of me
when you take in the simple sky
whose stars you name as if they were children.

Parable

The newborn pig could not unfold its legs
and from its palate a cleft
ending between the eyes blinded it.

Four neighbor boys came
throwing stones they'd chosen
from the cornfield, and later,

a farmhand drew a warm bath
to wash the small pig's cuts
and drowned it.

Before the farmhand came,
before the boys with
coat pockets fattened with stones,

another boy came, an older boy,
and beneath a brittle sycamore
set out sheets of newspaper.

He lay there with the pig on his chest
and took its hooves between his hands,
and he rubbed the hooves

as if the hooves were cold.
You're like a cat, he said to the pig.
You're like a sleeping dog, and

the pig, who may have wanted to believe
it was a cat, or a sleeping dog,
kissed the boy

with its damp nose.
The boy slept,
sometimes waking

to feel the four stones
of pig's feet, milk-warm and cleft.
The open-mouthed pig for a while slept too.

North Florida

A rooster drifts
into the neighborhood, and now
the cats are all
indoor cats. It's the rainy season
anyway, which means
every midafternoon we're aggressively
relieved of our misery,
then returned to it. My orange
tree in particular suffers:
the downpours keep thieving
its fruit. Once,
that was my work, though
at first I thought my orange
tree was a lemon tree,
would populate my kitchen
with meager green ovals
that didn't ever change color.
I flamed God, kept harvesting.
Then gave up. Then received
my fruitful, neglected bounty,
my lion's honey,
hallelujah. Now this
rooster's occupied my neighbor's
satellite dish, and I can
no longer pirate his HBO.
For this God can do
nothing. My other neighbor

tried, for which the rooster
sliced her to the elbows.
Afternoons on their closed porch,
her daughter plays doctor,
dabbing the scars with bubble mix.
Mornings, I check myself
for bruises from the night
before, wash out my wineglass
and tell jokes to the kitchen,
slipping naked into my tiny bathrobe,
dusting the scratched furniture
whose poky edges foul me. I drink
healing teas and think, *If I were a drag queen*
I'd go by Mary Rich. Everywhere,
cat heads dawdle in windows,
hard oranges on the sills.

Stray

i

It mostly seems unfashionable for the living to talk
for long about death, as if their meanwhile
invincibility were a shameful type of privilege—
this is the shallow

kind of thinking I made, wrapped in a dissolving
family quilt, having badly climbed a lesser sea stack
this morning on the coast, and only because I was
bored with the morning, which had consisted
otherwise of dancing to pop radio and eating peanut
butter. Vacations shouldn't have mornings,

but from my skinny sea stack, I felt at last a little
mighty, admiring what of the landscape, in a
raggedy fog, I could see, offshore roilings like
unaccountable self-losses and -gains, the whitecaps'
snowy logic seeming nothing more than the sea

fleeing the sea, and then the sea giving the sea back
to itself. Dying, I hope, is something like that.

ii

Like cradling a stray
you never had a name for,
its nipples

obtruded, both your necks
bent in adoration,
the body itself

threaded like spiral cases
and shafts, sinews exact,
my obedience

the ball bearings of it all,
as if saying yes to it,
sure, little life, little living,

yes, but, and—little gift
I never asked for, I'll one day
set you out on the lawn.

Goatfeathers

All morning, this skinny goat
stood idling in the drive,
cleaning its feathers
the way a child might
scrape flesh from an artichoke
if this child had never
eaten an artichoke. This goat
seemed surprised it had feathers at all.
And I was, I felt validly, surprised,

but my beloved was not:
he didn't mind this feathered goat,
bringing it milk and tying
around the goat's neck
a scarf, instead of,
as I would have, a leash,
so that I could keep it
to convince others there was once
a sudden goat in the drive,

and that the goat was feathered
like some kind of Jurassic
dog, or maybe Satan's
favorite idiot chicken,
but my beloved, my beloved
brought it milk and a scarf,

my scarf, which the goat, by noon,
pilled with slow licks,
and let fall, and forgot.

Six Valedictions from the Last Night I Loved You

For the band of panicked street cats
     lapping spoiled soup I'd discarded
         at the base of what I only knew
   to call a Mexican rose, and for you,
      dawdling on the lawn, bent over
         a Walmart telescope, in search of
stars that are remotest—Andromeda's
         cities, the vaporous
       shimmering that was the first star
   of Ophiuchus, which even by then was gone,

*

As if I were looking only to neglect that we were all
     we had, as we neglected those furry, gray
fungus gnats overrunning the bathroom, delicate sadnesses
     switching on and off against the illuminated mirror,

*

Remembering the gnats bred in the red pot of succulents—
     they seemed drawn to it, its color—
       and that I'd scoured unswept corners
   behind our refrigerator
      for a thin, nearly translucent cellar spider
       whose irretrievable webbing
        had accumulated dust,

and how I lifted the spider as I'd seen wading worshippers
      dredge water from the basin of a river,
              and how the spider didn't bother
      even to nip or scramble until I set him free,
           with great dignity,
                  in the jade plant's branches
              to eat,

             *

All I know of devotion
      being a man I meant to love better,
as he unlatched his bicycle from the chain-link
      to join, for the last time, the northbound traffic,
the stars, being disproportionate and few,
          marking his transportation
          through dim clusters of failures,

             *

Because Earth travels
      by a calculable series of truths that seem to have
          fallen simply, clumsily
into place,

             *

Forgive me
if the self is best

                      when falling out of love

                      with the self,

Colloquy with Creeper and Beer

All things bare but pine and pine-scaling creeper,
having dashed open in February fists of rolled leaves

to a light so plentiful it's worthless. The sun knows
to regain its worth through disappearance, and you

emerge from your cinderblock apartment
to hike to the gas station down the highway.

You haven't believed in good men in months,
but even the fists of creeper remaking the landscape

seem to you like a race between brothers.
Today is an anniversary: 1997, February,

across Hartwell, your neighbor's student, a freshman,
walked the tracks on a timber truss

spanning a narrow in the lake. Enough booze,
and no one hears a train: the student turned back

and was, it seemed to him, touched on the shoulder
as if by a friend, a word came to him, and he

pulled apart like a wishbone. Three days after this,
it was still February 1997, and you were standing

in an alfalfa field, scanning what you were to shoot:
the neighbor's emptied Schlitz cans,

a precise row of silver-and-white
he'd set out on a rotted hay bale.

He laid his rifle, its forestock flattening the weeds,
across the ledge of a shallow ditch.

Because you were small, you stood up into the rifle.
Leaning against your back a bit, he pressed

your shoulder into the rifle, and you pointed it at a can
and pulled. *Good*, he kept saying,

and he set himself into you, he took your hands
to the trigger and had you pull again, with him,

rifle sound crackling against blank trees
and returning to you. *Good*, he said, and he fired again,

and you took each dig of the rifle into your giving shoulder—
and because you wanted to believe this was good,

you kept it to yourself, kept even from yelling
at this man who wanted

to gather you, to remake you
into what may have been worth a man.

Onto the highway, the gas station lets fall
narrow strafings of fluorescent light

by which small cars are touched as they clip past,
and you might look up to it,

you might ask to be given a part in the dialogue
between light and bodies passing through it,

between the voice that begins in the throat
and the voice a mouth abandons.

Tonight is not the night you'll step into the light
of traffic. The rain is soft and good,

and the wind is bitter. Even if you could talk it into
coming gently against you, as if,

in this space, the wind could come close
to holding you, still you'll say the wind itself is bitter.

Game

He said, let's play a game.

Imagine a party, he said,

you're drinking, and we share

a daughter. I'm worried, I can't

find her, he said, and you're

too far gone. So we're in love,

I said, and he said, No,

it doesn't have to be like that.

We're in love, I said. And

we played the game, and we were.

A Little Learning

Eddie used to touch her men
like this: *Deep down*, she said.
We all wanted what she had,
all the evidence she'd collected
on love between bodies.
Many would have paid for it
and believed anything:
A real man keeps his pocket watch
in the folds of his heart.
Anything that opens is a mouth,
any mouth will swallow you up.
Even now, I believe
that to make a person love you,
you just have to do the trick right,
follow a certain order maybe,
or add a clap of the hands,
some sort of hocus-pocus,
and his mouth will open to you
like a cupboard, again and again.
Prick yourself on a spindle,
you'll die with no one.
Prick yourself on a compass,
they'll come to you in droves.
Eddie loved the one who came to her
in eleventh grade, moved downriver
with a herd of fainting goats
to the deep country where

the galaxy's arms cast pollen
across the barely visible Blue Ridge.
Goat liver keeps the Devil
off your heart, she told me,
stooped by the rec center bleachers
we'd snuck to after her husband's
funeral to smoke. *Tobacco takes down*
a swelling if you have one, she said.
And then, *A cup of vinegar*
under our bed meant
we never did get in the family way.
I haven't seen Eddie.
Coming home holidays, I take
the county highway north, a narrow
road along a stretch of river
that brings me up
between Six Mile and Newry.
I keep an eye for goats
but never really find any,
just cornstalk stubble in cracked soil
and power lines
humming work songs for no one.
Those drives, any figure I see is Eddie.
Any story is true.
Anything that opens is a mouth.
A fox means a rainstorm.
A cat means a death. A deer means
I wasn't looking hard enough.

Love Poem against the Body

This man I'm seeing thinks his nipples are baby-
grape-shaped and pale as two sun-faded pencil-top

erasers, and he doesn't like when I question
or bite them. Our first date, we split pork nachos

after he apologized that his fingertips were flaked
with dead skin: he sucks on them. He sucks on all of them,

all at once, and fairly crankily, like a toddler gobbling
a corncob. He has blood that thickens as if he's sick,

and special machines, and hypertension meds
he sucks down. This man asks, inspecting my nipples

with a dying thumbprint, *What about yourself do you hate
most? The blood? Brain? Eyeballs? Bowels?* We sleep

in a snarl, like lovers found in snow.

Threesome with Sea Monsters and Theft

Starfish between them
fatten on tube worms
trapped in the tide pool

rock gardens. Dressed
like a schoolboy, the one mopes
up to Devils Churn.

The other follows. The sea,
caught in the cave's throat,
throws our voices back to us,

so the one lowers his head
into the Churn, yells.
The other moves shoreward,

where, underfoot, razor clams
closed against him
fracture and crumb.

Anywhere he steps,
he is breaking some.
Fagged crows preen,

gobbling fleas.
An opened crab's hand
brings down gulls.

The one boy's hands
are rough as silt.
He signals we sit.

He touches the other's jaw
with his blue fingers.
Each believes he is a net

trapped in another
net's arms. A strand
of the one's unwashed hair

sticks in a hinge
of the other's spectacles.
I am here. I loosen it.

Sea monster on sea monster
drowning, rock pools break
the sea that thieves

wrecked shells away
as sediment.
All of us are soon gone.

The waves go out and out.
I am just another thing
that loves them.

Nemean Lion

Flaying him, all
smeared hair

and pelt-plate,
I forgot

the olive tree
and club. Forgot

the crushed
throat's bristling,

the thistle flowers,
fruit I picked

from unmanageable
thornbushes.

Forgot the quivers
of arrows

I needed to
feel his skin,

to know it,
to find skin

for what skin is
made of.

But I'll remember
the skinning,

the tilt
and roughness

of the lion's claw
against the lion—

Flaying him,
freed there

in the closed
cave, with all

that cat meat,
bound

to a hermitage
of skins,

some way myself
in him—

I knew
to hold him

with me: how,
saying *Love*,

I am saying
always *Him*,

and him,
and him—

Through Him, and with Him, and in Him

When the clothes began to smell curdled, almost sweet,

my father loosened the dryer's flex hose, and the houseflies

and the dead skunk kit slipped from the wall's mouth.

We watched the flies relinquish it, orbit away, return

to scale the galled face as a sort of living, woolen

hood—wringing their hands, mining the kit

with stylet-like, palp-flaring snouts, dissolving crusts

to suck from the cheeks—*Servant, whom we have called today . . .*

To them, from the distance between us, extending

my giant hand, I'd have been an offering, a body to section:

Argus-eyed as they are, they see nothing of God

and are unworried. Always the meat on the rib beneath

the binding shield of the sternum. Always houseflies

busying themselves with their knack for the dead,

their furred bellies twitching like the flanks of a cow.

Body of my body—Father: it isn't always true that a good son

dies and a bad one punishes his father by living. Before

you buried the kit out in the yard, you helped me bathe it.

Parable

A sycamore overlooks
a canal and a field of brittle corn
where against the cropland backdrop

a house far-off grays yearly, smoke
from bonfires of trimmings and rot often

blackening any vantage of the white-crowned
Dolomites. On this day,
no bonfires. A local boy stripped

and lowered himself
to swim in the canal and was sunk.

Ask him, and he'll say he remembers
only the now old sycamore, its split roots
tapping, standing there, grown

still against the Dolomites' stillness,

and his hands' nailbeds then
naked and blushing,

his father dressing them with kisses
and praying under the blue, bent
light of Bartholomew, fixed in glass.

Ask him: his own ceremonies

have since seemed less—cotton balls
soaked with witch hazel

he holds to what of himself he can see
with a small mirror.
As if by a tightening of thread, he closes himself

to purify, after men are rough,
what he has been given.

As when Samuel poured a vial of oil
over the head of aimless Saul

and kissed him,

and this opened the eyes of God to Saul,
and God bent in from the gray morning sky
to watch.

Even the sycamore's heard the story:
Saul was given
a drove of donkeys,

the oak of Tabor, the goatherd
driving his tribe across
the terebinth woodland of Judea,

the gracious stranger who offered Saul
the bread he carried in his arms.

Ask the sycamore how the parable
moves, and he'll tell you: imprinted,

reprinted in small, determined
histories—the boy in the canal, scanning
the water's undersurface,

the long, untraceable refraction
glittering with handfuls of erupted light,

and sycamore seedlings,
helicoptering down, out of the inevitable air.

Ars Poetica

For a night
he tapped
like the Devil

at my window,

like he wanted
returned

something I'd stolen.

Ars Poetica for the Devil

For a night
he tapped
like the Devil

at my window,

like he wanted
returned

something I'd stolen.

Or maybe
he was only
a tree, lurching

in a windstorm—

This poem
was a tree

or the Devil,

tapping, and
in his hands
were choughs

dropping

gravel they mistook
for pecans.

I counted

the lightning's
distance,
turning, in

my open hand,

picked pecans, and
with the other

sketching the bare-handed

Devil, alone now
the thunder'd driven
away his birds—

This was when

the poem was
his sweetest:

the Devil

standing in
his field,
looking as if

he'd lost

four birds
and suddenly

was without

anything else
to do.
I drew

a salt circle

around my bed
and slept,

finally.

What else could
I have done?
This poem

was a tree,

a chough
in the hand,

or

he was
a bare hand—
and

what else is

a bare hand
but the Devil's,

tapping?

What else is
a poem
to him

as he goes

but
the thunder

of his leaving

and the thunder
that drove
away

those stupid birds

he once
loved?

Panacea, Florida

i

Even rhododendron
groves are called
hells; bait towns

are called Panacea.
I'd come to set myself
at the foot of the first god

I found, but the closest I came
were forests of fat-trunked
bald cypresses daintily

submerged at the roots, each
seeming, even clustered,
somehow lonely and content.

ii

Afternoons, a friend
and I walked through the inland
national forest,

Katy touching open-mouthed
pitcher plants or braiding her hair
with weeds and lantern flowers,

both of us leaving
handprints in a silt beach
made less erodible

by carefully placed, halved
flat tires, and
I didn't really question it:

planting our hands like that, so
simply, erodibly,
as if we were nothing,

admiring ourselves for it—
or that we vowed to continue
as a kind of abbreviated

pilgrimage to Two Blondes,
the nearby liquor store,
collecting on the way

three or four abandoned
nests, one shapeless
and unfinished, another like

a small bear's heart stuck
with fur, some months ago
broken suddenly.

Katy said we could keep
our sadnesses in these,
deposit them between twigs

as rolled hexes
written on coupon scraps,
burn the nests before leaving.

iii

I began taking more walks
alone, studying crooked pelicans
perched in a small bay harbor

for signs of anything ancient
or saintly. I thought healing
should come to me obviously,

a gaggle of trees
bumbling out of the sea,
each trimmed with

barnacles, each eely root
setting itself at my feet
and never getting up again.

Love Poem So Tall It Ends in Heaven

A man I loved kept a folded square
of masking tape in his pocket
He did this   / only for a year
His masking tape was bright
orange and fraying   As evidence
/ coroners had used it to attach
to his father's calf the rope
his father'd used   / This man
planted the tape in our yard
when the year was done and
from it grew thirteen beams   /
From these beams rafters grew
Ropes uncurled from these rafters
and fathers hanged from the ropes
/ Over the fathers a roof
blossomed like a shield
and against it a ladder leaned   /
The ladder was so tall
the man I loved said it must
have ended in heaven   And down
/ from the ladder an angel scurried
while we slept   In its mouth
it carried torn strips   / of tape
The angel pressed this tape
on the calves of the man I loved
like bandages   / Each morning
I removed the tape   I was careful

not to wake him   Each morning
/ he'd walk through the garden
of swaying fathers   He'd kneel
beside our rosemary bush   / He'd
rub its leaves in his hands   He'd ball
his hands in his hair to scent it   / He
wanted   / just   to   keep
his earthliness with him   / In hell
this is the only prerequisite

The Man Who Fell in Love with the Moon

In the hours before Lewiston, driving the Gorge
on the slower, Washington side, I listened

to *The Odyssey* on tape: Telemachus borrowing
his own black boat, the murderous suitors in pursuit.

Wheat hills in the Gorge looked like clumped
sand dunes, miles-long tracks crossing them all

as if war tanks had torn through.
I always want to see the landscape as invaded:

how Mars becomes suddenly visible even in light,
or, in the Gorge, light itself

casting wind-turbine shadows across sage mountains
like stiff fingers thieving without profit.

Odysseus is in Ogygia. *Ogygia.* What
a stupid little word. As is *Ringleb*, which sounds

like a persistent foot infection. And my father—
I try to imagine white sand, a coastal cottage

in the west of Sicily, a wife picking wild rocket
he's planted in the lawn, and evenings he brings

fresh urchins in a small, black mesh bag he carries
with him always to the sea. She cleans

the urchins of white sand, and together they cook,
quietly, because they are so in love.

Tonight, I bought two bottles of Cook's
from the only Safeway in Lewiston,

and now, filling gluey, plastic sacks
with machine ice, I work to cool them quickly

in a motel mini fridge, which won't close
without my duffel propped against it. Waiting,

I watch an old video of Alan Shepard hitting golf balls
on the moon, golf balls that could have flown

for miles before landing in white sand, grains of
which for a short time might have floated, suspended

like miniature, orbitless planets. It is a stupid thing to say
my father enjoys golfing, but I'll say he does.

I'll say he is sad. Or in love. I'll say he is lonelier
than all those stupid little golf balls on the moon.

Ode for Dark Matter

Watching animal
silhouettes in darkness

shift, I feel attended
though I'm alone:

I think I'll be
ambushed by possums

I often see
nosing the compost

and retreat to bed
with a faintheartedness

jump-started by nothing.
Thirty years, and still

I'll believe
I am shepherded

by the invisible—
which is,

after all, all
around: blank motes

lashing me to action.
Tonight, I'll eat

a plateful of shortbread
and dream—possums, probably—

wrapped in the pilled blanket,
the body sleeping

like a tree, slow
like a tree.

It's almost a heaven,
neglecting you.

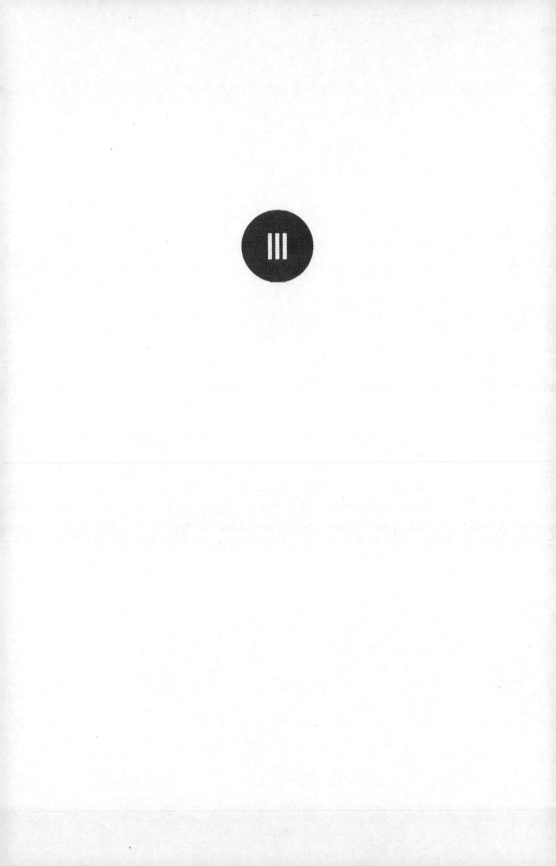

A Wedding of Jackals

i. My father's garden

The way of saying *I cannot help you* in Italian being sometimes *This does not serve me*, I offer a small bribe to the clerk at the Treviso cadastral office in exchange for my father's address.

I'm told he lives in the municipality of Asolo, only an hour north by car. Arriving in nearby Possagno at dinner, I eat on the Temple of Canova's stairs what my stomach allows from a Ziploc of salted sardines. The moon is ringed, the Grappa massif overtaken by low clouds: snow. I wait in the fusty rental car—licorice, maybe, and old luggage leather—until I assume my father is sleeping, then I make my way up his narrow farming road.

My father's villa is unlit, larger than I'd thought, and I climb the gate, boosting myself from the lip of an empty fountain whose lion's head, the mouth obstructed, spills nothing. Inside the gate, no cars. No one home, nothing shifting in the manicured juniper hedges wrapping the drive.

Snow all around me in my father's garden—*Tomorrow*, I promise myself, *I'll find his workplace and call, pretending to be someone I am not, to see when he'll arrive home.*

ii. After a night at sea

Each year, before his birthday in the late summer, my father would fly in, from Venice, from Munich, to stay a week in an inn on Lake Hartwell. He would visit most afternoons, after doctors' appointments or meetings at the university, and he would endure American movies playing in one of Seneca's handful of stadium theaters. We would eat what he missed most—hamburgers, generally, and steaks.

He smelled always of black pepper, which he ate with everything—it wasn't from eating pepper, the smell, but something innate, something in the blood maybe: I smell it on myself, sometimes, and leave it to my undershirts and bed.

From a local marina surrounded by farms of Carolina Reapers, my father and I rented a pontoon boat, and we spent the day on Hartwell. We took off our shirts in the sun. I slept sweating on the plastic benches while my father followed other boats through the maze of identical inlets.

He pronounced us lost by sundown, and in the black he spotlighted docks in case someone was there to help. It took until the early morning to arrive home after what seemed like a night at sea, surrounded by black hills, black water.

iii. Segestana

Beside my father's hotel in Bonagia, a small bay is crowded with fishing boats and faded dories. Old crewmen stand shirtless in the unusual winter sun. The Via Lungomare is empty except for a few cars, and I find a space in front of the hotel Saverino, park, and wait. Two guests leave the hotel within an hour, and the manager of the hotel restaurant eventually comes to ask me what my business is on the Lungomare.

I park again on the provincial road east of Bonagia, my car pointed toward the village center. I study the face of each man who passes by. I never see my father.

Halfway into the next morning, I sit alone in the car, humming along to American songs as they play on a local Trapani station. I grow restless. For the remainder of the day I choose certain men, men who most resemble my father, and I follow them. *For practice*, I promise myself.

One man I follow to a laundromat in the village of Crocefissello; another drives to a large apartment complex in the west of Trapani; a final man—I am sure for a long time that he is my father—drives with a woman and a small girl all the way to Calatafimi-Segesta. *A sister*, I keep saying, but when they pull into the parking lot of a trattoria, I see the man's face clearly, and I curse myself for having said it at all.

I wait for them to finish their lunch and then follow them to the Elymian city of Segesta. It begins to rain softly, almost pleasantly. I track the family—six legs under a large, red umbrella—as they wander through Segesta's roofless Doric temple. And then they're gone: following a path up its mild slope toward the forest, the family disappears in the mist. They'd been moving in the direction of an amphitheater built, a sign in the parking lot says, *after an invasion of treacherous Greeks.*

iv. Urchins

The next afternoon is clear enough that the shallows near the coastline are illuminated, precise urchins shimmering from the undersides of the coastal stones. East of Bonagia, I follow a path to find gloved, barefoot children collecting urchins and carrying them back to a chum bucket filled with seawater. An elderly Sicilian woman sits there, a cutting board on her lap stained bright orange, turning the spiny hulls in her hand.

She asks me if I'd like three or four, *to take home*, but I tell her I wouldn't know what to do with them. She has me sit and teaches me to shuck urchins.

After dusk, I drive to my post on the provincial road. A rainstorm from the mainland makes any sighting of my father impossible, so I put on a raincoat and walk Via Lungomare. I stand across from the Saverino, its restaurant the only lit building on the coastal strip. The same manager is inside now, carrying wine bottles from one corner of the restaurant to the other. Cleanly dressed men emerge from the kitchen delivering whole fish cooked under mounds of salt, and the patrons laugh while breaking the encasements with souvenir picks. Sitting next to an old, portable television that plays the news, a man with a white napkin tucked into his dress shirt turns to hail a passing waiter.

I remove my hood to better see the face of my illuminated father and then flee up the narrow road toward my rented car.

v. Over a drink at the Otto e Mezzo Lounge Bar

It was early in the summer when my father last visited. Each afternoon, small windstorms stirred the parking lot with scraps from white-flowering rows of myrtles. My mother having shown him, *at last*, the porn I'd printed out to keep, my father pushed past me in the narrow foyer to sit alone in the rented car he'd parked on the road. I watched from the den's window. Maybe twenty minutes passed, and he drove off.

I called the inn the next day and was told he'd gone. There's little else to say. In gay bars the size of double-wides, men would tell me their brutal stories, and I'd tell them my father bunched the papers into a wad and stuffed them in my mouth. I'd say he dragged me by the legs through the parking lot, my hair sweeping up flowers. But nothing happened, really. My father came and left, and I called over a group of friends to go swimming.

We rowed out to the top of an old timber truss bridge exposed in the low of the lake. We played at touching rooftops from the drowned city, but only ever found the bell tower. Then we sank, touching it with our feet. Not even the boy who surfaced squealing, splinters caught in his toes, was me.

vi. A dog in the wheel

An exultation of passion and strength, the sign says of the *Mountain of Salt*, but the mountain is hardly a mountain, and the salt is not salt. The mountain is a hill small enough to fit on the stage of a theater, and it is made of cement, and trapped in the cement are thirty stiff-legged, wooden horses. The *Mountain of Salt* sits on the slope of a ridge along the border of Gibellina Nuova. From this vantage, I see my father limping through empty streets of the abandoned town, stopping along the way to take in the art cemented into the walls of its buildings. A matted dog tracks him and the woman holding on to him. She hisses at the dog when it comes close, and the dog skitters away only to close the distance again after enough time passes.

A series of stray showers comes in from the west, sending me back to the rental car to pick at a loaf of bread and wait. When the rains pass, I drive through the city to find him.

Rounding the corner of the central piazza, I brake suddenly as the dog, rain-slicked now, darts beneath my wheel. Meters to my right, my father's wife comes running from under an archway, spitting strong, hateful words, and I tear away, dragging the dog along the cobbled road.

Gibellina Vecchia is nearly twelve kilometers east of the new city. Only ruins—less than ruins: slabs of poured concrete indicating the leveled city's street plans. A gang of bustards, as I watch them, picks insects from the concrete's thistles and moss. Above me, birds I cannot see to name call out to one another in their barren language.

71

vii. Temple of Venus

The Sicilian coast darkens, shrinks away each year from the sea's beatings and gall, and each day the seaboard fog brought on by the morning shreds, displaced, with the passing through of rock pigeons. By midafternoon the sun burns fog and everything else, it seems, away— but me, I think there are words, at least, yet to distill and swallow. Sunday, my father at Mass in the Parrocchia Maria, I stand at a food cart in white, seemingly unretractable light and wait to place my order of poached fish on rice. *I will be his.* I say this again and again.

I say it to the small, outlying winds the sirocco sheds and forgets over Favignana and Levanzo. I tell it to the cactuses of Bonagia and the grapes of Mozia and the stilled windmills overlooking the salt pans east of Trapani. I drink bathtub fragolino in the backseat of my rented car and say it to my pinkish visions. Touched as if by the donas de fuera, I use the words to lure urchins' spines from my feet, and the black calcium melts away like wax. My last day in Sicily, I say it to the morning, and the morning chides me with sunlight and rain, which to some Sicilians means a nearby wedding of jackals, though there are no jackals in Sicily. That afternoon I follow my father up the mountain road to Erice.

He curves back, again and again, against the violent switches, and I follow him. He overtakes a black platform truck loaded with crated chickens on the straight, ancient road where the last Mediterranean vantage before the summit is blackened by frayed salt cedars, and

I follow him. Above us, a cloud swallows the mountain. My father moves on, and around him the cloud splits, my father a word in the mouth, and then the cloud closes back on itself, and I follow him.

IV

Peacock at a Garden Party

All the Fiats
have clambered up the hill
on the old Roman road—

Reformed, it translates—
and in shallow ditches lining the villa
have parked nose-first.

Their owners, skinny-suited
Slovenes and Italian
Northern Leaguers,

orange-cheeked and already
in their wine, go
slipping up the hill. I am in

my father's garden
holding a tray of undercooked,
clean-cut pigeon breasts

skewered top to bottom.
There's talk of a wild peacock
none of us has seen.

It cries like a child
from the bordering thicket
while I make new rounds

with a tray of potato dumplings,
dainty mouthfuls: the yellow dumpling
like an allergic eye,

flushing with clusters of meat;
the bitter green;
the pink one, lidded and sweet.

I am in my father's garden
in a silk-lined suit
and a thin, European tie,

watching two young boys—
Umberto and Lorenzo,
I think they are called—

dig a limb of charcoal
from the outlying grill.
Umberto drags black lines

beneath Lorenzo's eyes, arms
himself with a stick, and both boys
disappear down the hill.

Our wailing peacock quiets and hides.
I am in my father's garden
where a south wind runs off

with the sun. My father
tries to ruffle my clippered hair.
Here we are: love, it seems,

is a lack of alternatives.
The pride-and-joy
cottonwoods, flaring

hierarchies of branches,
flap their papery leaves.
Underneath a juniper hedge,

the peacock folds and flattens
its plumage of doped, bright eyes
and holds its breath.

Love Poem

Imagine
a day alone
and call it *Love*.

Let it mean
All things are equal.
Let it mean

you have eaten,
you are *Filled*
by an assortment

of quick-sale meats.
Use the word
Delicious.

For yourself,
use the word *Collected.*
Complete.

Let it mean
All things revolve around
a wet, living stone.

Call it
Heart. Let it mean
that Earth

moves with you,
loop after loop.
Never mind

what you are
known for
or last night's dinner

of cheese bread.
What is sadness?
Think, *Sadness*

was a friend
across the table.
Never mind

the man
she named for you
over dinner on Friday.

What was his name?
Anthony?
Never mind

Anthony. Anthony
is blond
and blue-eyed

and a waiter
and, it's said,
quite funny.

Think, *Anthony is not*
a day alone though,
not Love.

Let this
break your heart,
but don't say

Break your heart
here or anywhere.
Nobody wants to see it

wild and out.
In this poem,
ask *What heart?*

Let it be
the wet, living stone.
Revolve around it

this way:
Alone and *Alive.*
Remember

you are equal to
anything equal to
the earth.

Say *Little heart,*
for all your murmuring,
I imagine

you're textured like
a persimmon.
Say *Little heart,*

if you are
at all
like a persimmon,

I'll seal you
in a jar
of limewater

to rid you
of your unbearable flavor.
Say *Little heart,*

which of your ventricles
is your favorite,
your hardest worker?

Drop your little heart
in a mason jar
and set it aside for the day.

You will be
truly in *Love* then,
won't you?

You will be
Complete?
This poem won't mind

what you're known for
or what you've brought
with you.

Nobody will love you
like this poem does.
Let this poem

fill you. Let it
wash your hair.
It will use

egg whites
and honey.
Maybe you'd like

something different.
Tell this poem
what you want.

Anything.
This Earth.
Say *Little heart,*

let me
thumb you through
until all your stones

are turned and
all your meats sold.
Say *Little heart,*

let there be
a primacy in you.
Let there be

a primacy in you
a poem
can get to.

Self-Portrait as Medusa in Shock

Medusa being the Italian word for, of all things, jellyfish—precious,
  fleshy poison sacs,

the sea's white spit: as if Perseus had released the severed head back
  into the water, and the head had burst, metamorphosed, like a
  kind of Christian remorse,

into a swarm of these upside-down, dunce-faced nothings; dotted
  and rootless sea-trees; the gods' hungriest, most unloved children.

And though I never loved the stories where turning a mirror on a thing

cured it of itself, I did love the stories of delivery and return: Jonah,
  cracked from the whale's skull, or Jesus, cracked from the cave,

and Lazarus, and the prodigal, racked with guilt,

and even Eve-like Medusa, if only in a mirror-shield, cracked, and
  from her neck, from the interior, spilled a golden giant and a
  winged horse; imagine that—

the impossible shock, I like to think, of color. *Impossibility* being any
  god's word

for *Love*—that other precious, fleshy poison.

When I allow myself, in stories, to return to a point of origin, the way
    souls drag with them their finite bodily sadnesses if they return
    to heaven,

the stories always recount the returns I have made to my own father.

In my versions of heaven—my father's

rented boat off the coast in the Sicilian north, say—I struggle always to
    climb aboard, and in that struggle I am kissed above the right elbow

by a *medusa*. And my father, outraged by this offense—

and though he can afford to be stung by nothing, as a bee or red ant or
    jellyfish would stop his heart—arms himself with his wife's

snorkel gear, and for a half hour circles the boat to snatch up, in a net
    you might use to scoop dead goldfish from their bowls,

all the jellyfish he can find, turning them out to slowly die on the
    spackled deck next to the boat's ladder.

It seems a father can work to keep his children from the world's injuries,

but rarely his own—the way, in anaphylaxis, when a sting felt again is
    tremendous enough, even the body's healing turns an accidental
    mirror on itself

and irreparably cracks. This, in the stories of seeing the self, is the shock that makes any return to it impossible:

from the interior, a healing so great it petrifies the heart for good.

NOTES

"My Husband, Lost in the Wild": The title of this poem is adapted from the title of the Beirut song "My Wife, Lost in the Wild," which can be found on the EP *Realpeople: Holland*.

"Mutius in the Garden of Rejection": In Shakespeare's *Titus Andronicus*, Mutius intends to safeguard a sibling's love that is deemed illegal by his father and Rome. The quoted line in the epigraph of this poem becomes ironic in the play when, trying to fulfill it, Mutius is murdered by his father.

"Parable" (The newborn pig could not unfold its legs): The lines "*You're like a cat*, he said to the pig. / *You're like a sleeping dog*" are adapted from lines in Deborah Digges's poem "Nursing the Hamster."

"Colloquy with Creeper and Beer": The phrase "a light so plentiful it's worthless" is adapted from the line "Into the sunlight, worthless and every-where" from Charles Wright's poem "Lonesome Pine Special." The line "You haven't believed in good men in months" is in conversation with Larry Levis's line "Because you haven't praised anything in months," which begins his poem "The Spirit Says, You Are Nothing."

"Love Poem against the Body": The last line of this poem is inspired by Eavan Boland's poem "Quarantine."

"Threesome with Sea Monsters and Theft": Devils Churn is a small inlet and cave on the Oregon coast, near Florence. This poem began as an exercise in conversation with the work of other poets, and it owes a great deal to adaptation and borrowing. The sentence "He touches the other's jaw / with his blue fingers" is adapted from the line "You touch my knees with your blue fingers" in Ai's "Conversation," a poem for Robert Lowell. The sentence

"Each believes he is a net // trapped in another / net's arms" borrows from the third section of Robert Lowell's poem "Through the Night," the line "Sea monster on sea monster drowning" borrows from the fifth section of Robert Lowell's "Circles," and the line "The waves go out and out" borrows from Robert Lowell's "The Quaker Graveyard in Nantucket." The final sentence from the poem borrows from an unpublished poem by one of my closest childhood friends, Katy Ray.

"Nemean Lion": Murdering the Nemean lion is the first of Heracles's labors, a series of acts that Heracles undertakes out of penitence after he murders his wife and children.

"Through Him, and with Him, and in Him": The title of this poem borrows from Catholic eucharistic doxology; the phrase "Servant, whom we have called today" is adapted from language in Catholic Masses for the dead; and the phrase "Body of my body" references the biblical line "This is my body, which is given for you: this do in remembrance of me," which is attributed to Christ.

"The Man Who Fell in Love with the Moon": The title of this poem comes from a Tom Spanbauer novel of the same name. The images that end the poem were inspired by Erin Belieu's poem "The Man Who Fills in Space."

"A Wedding of Jackals": This sequence is inspired by Matsuo Bashō's *The Narrow Road to the Deep North*, Sophie Calle's *Suite vénitienne*, Eugenio Montale's *Cuttlefish Bones*, and, with my deepest gratitude, lessons from Garrett Hongo. The *Mountain of Salt* (*Montagna di Sale*) is an art installation by Mimmo Paladino. The slabs described in Gibellina Vecchia are part of the *Great Crack* (*Grande Cretto*), a land artwork by Alberto Burri.

"Peacock at a Garden Party": The phrase "love, it seems, // is a lack of alternatives" is adapted from the line "It seems courage is a lack of alternatives" from Deborah Digges's poem "The New World."

ACKNOWLEDGMENTS

I am deeply grateful to the editors of the following journals in which these poems, sometimes in other versions, first appeared:

The Adroit Journal: "Peacock at a Garden Party"

AGNI: "A Little Learning"

At Length: "Colloquy with Creeper and Beer" (as "Colloquy") and "Love Poem"

Gulf Coast: "Threesome with Sea Monsters and Theft"

The Hong Kong Review: "North Florida" (as "Florida")

The Journal: "Love Poem against the Body"

jubilat: "I Was, of Course" and "Parable" (The newborn pig could not unfold its legs)

Kenyon Review: "Love Poem to the Son My Father Wished For"

Nimrod International Journal of Prose and Poetry: "Ars Poetica for the Devil," "Mutius in the Garden of Rejection," and "Parable" (A sycamore overlooks)

Ploughshares: "Six Valedictions from the Last Night I Loved You"

Poetry: "Love Poem So Tall It Ends in Heaven," "My Husband, Lost in the Wild," and "A Wedding of Jackals"

Puerto del Sol: "Self-Portrait as Medusa in Shock"

Sixth Finch: "Ode for Dark Matter"

Tampa Review: "The Man Who Fell in Love with the Moon"

wildness: "Nemean Lion"

Kaveh Akbar, Daniel Anderson, Sherwin Bitsui, Lorena Burke, Maari Carter, Dorothy Chan, Katy Didden, Andrew Epstein, David Groff, Barbara Hamby, Robert Hass, Nancy Hauserman, Jessa Heath, Sarah Higgs, Martin Kavka, Barbara Kerr, James Kimbrell, David Kirby, Joanna Klink, Keith Kopka, Spencer Krauss, Laurel Lathrop, Paige Lewis, Ed Madden, Maurice Manning, Moriah McCarthy, Michael McDermit, Ray McManus, Charlotte Muzzi, Marilyn Nelson, Carl Phillips, Alycia Pirmohamed, Paige Quiñones, Natalie Shapero, Zack Strait, Ellen Bryant Voigt, and Mat Wenzel, thank you, thank you, thank you for the immense and loving generosity of your support and guidance.

Erin Belieu, Geri Doran, Garrett Hongo, Ed Madden, and Nancy Swanson, you have each given me so much of your time, and in that time you have helped me to better shape my writing and my life. You have my deepest gratitude for all that you have taught me. This book is for you, with my love and admiration.

Immense gratitude to the family at Tin House for bringing this book to life. David Caligiuri, Masie Cochran, Elizabeth DeMeo, Alex Gonzales, Becky Kraemer, Sangi Lama, Nanci McCloskey, Craig Popelars, Jakob Vala, and especially Alyssa Ogi, you've made real one of my wildest dreams, and I couldn't be more thankful for you.

These poems were completed with the generous support of Florida State University Creative Writing Program, the University of Oregon Creative Writing Program, the Bread Loaf Writers' Conference, Fishtrap, the *Kenyon Review* Writers Workshops, Lambda Literary, and the Sewanee Writers' Conference. Gratitude also to Mary Braun, Karen Ford, Miriam McFall Starlin, and the Academy of American Poets.

To my mother and father: thank you for loving me and for teaching me love.

Nikki Dodd, Katy Ray, and Sarah Stellwagen, you are my first sisters, my family, and I owe so much to your enduring kinship, devotion, and love.

Zach Linge, my heart, I am ecstatically outside of language with you.

JAYME RINGLEB is a queer writer raised in the southern United States and northern Italy. Jayme's poems have appeared recently in *Poetry*, *Kenyon Review*, *Gulf Coast*, and *Ploughshares*. An assistant professor of English at Meredith College, Jayme lives in Raleigh, North Carolina.